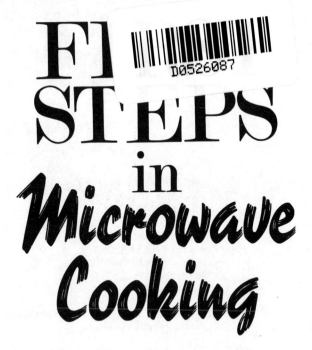

FIRST STEPS in Microwave Cooking

Jan Harris

INKLON PUBLICATIONS
SOUTHAMPTON

Published by Inklon Publications.
Shamrock Quay, William Street,
Southampton SO1 1QL.

First published 1981
Reprinted 1982, 1983, 1984
Second edition published 1985
Reprinted 1986, 1987
Third edition published 1987

Braille edition available from Hampshire Braille Transcription Service, 10 Crabwood Drive, West End, Southampton, Hampshire.

ISBN 0 9507618 6 9

Edited by **Angus Waycott**
Designed and produced by
Tony Fast Graphic, Southampton.
Illustrations **Paul Haynes**

Printed in Great Britain by J. W. Arrowsmith Ltd., Bristol

CONTENTS

PART 1

Basic
Information

Welcome to Microwave Cooking

However much you enjoy cooking, there's a limit to how much time you want to spend on it. Sometimes, of course, it's a pleasure to serve up an excellent meal which has taken many hours, or even days, to prepare, but there are also days when even cooking for oneself can be a tiresome chore, let alone having to provide for others.

Unfortunately for the cook, time spent in the kitchen is rarely a matter of choice. It depends on what you're cooking — and how many people are waiting to eat it.

What's really needed, then, to rescue the cook from "slaving for hours over a hot stove" is a change in the method of cooking itself — and that's just what a microwave oven provides. Suddenly, food takes a half, a quarter, or even less, of its usual cooking time. And there are plenty of other advantages besides speed:

— A microwave oven is much more energy-efficient than a conventional cooker, which means that you'll use less electricity.

— There's less washing up to be done, because food can be eaten from the same dish it's cooked in.

— Defrosting frozen food becomes a matter of minutes rather than hours.

— You can reheat leftovers in seconds, without drying them out.

— Food cooked by microwave retains more of its natural colour, flavour and nutritional value.

— Cooking is cooler, cleaner and freer from odours than before.

— Small quantities of food can be cooked very economically — a big benefit for people who live alone.

— A microwave oven can be used anywhere: in the kitchen, in a bedroom, or even out of doors (with a suitable extension lead).

— A microwave oven does more than just cook, defrost and reheat. It can dry herbs, melt gelatine, soften butter, sterilize baby bottles and much more (see "Useful Tips" on page 31).

But is microwave cooking easy?

Like driving a car, darning a sock or any other skill, the answer is "Yes, it's easy — once you've learned how." That's why it's important, before you get going on your favorite Cordon Bleu recipes, to master the basic techniques of microwave cooking and the way they differ from conventional cooking methods. Better, too, to practise on simple, inexpensive foods rather than make your first errors on a pound of best fillet steak!

This book aims to teach you those basic techniques, explaining how a microwave oven works, how to use it and how to look after it.

The practical sections contain lists and recipes using some of the most commonly-chosen food items, with detailed instructions on how to prepare them the microwave way. These lists are not intented to be exhaustive, still less a guide to gourmet eating. What they provide is a training ground — a basis on which to get started.

Naturally, you don't have to take the suggestions in any particular order; pick them out as you like, trying the ones you fancy. It's a good idea to begin by using your microwave oven in conjunction with your conventional cooker; make part of the meal in the microwave, and the rest in the usual way. And well before you've tried every suggestion in this book, you will have begun to acquire the confidence and the experience to go on to more complicated dishes. You won't have to ask yourself — as you will at the beginning — "How long do I cook *this* for?" You'll have a "feel" for the answer already; it will have started to become instinctive.

And when that happens, it means that the microwave revolution is really under way in your household. Enjoy it? You'll wonder how on earth you used to manage without it.

How a Microwave Oven Works

Although it sounds as if it ought to be complicated, the way a microwave oven works is really quite simple.

Microwaves themselves are just high-frequency radio waves — little pulses of energy. These waves are already part of nearly everyone's daily experience: television broadcasts and long-distance telephone calls for instance, are transmitted by them.

One of the oven's main components is the *magnetron*, which transforms ordinary electrical current into microwaves. As it does so, the magnetron releases the microwaves into the oven, where they reflect off the metal walls and enter the food, agitating the moisture molecules within it. This causes friction; friction produces heat; and the heat cooks the food. The high speed of cooking is because of the very fast rate at which the moisture molecules are agitated — nearly 2500 million cycles per second.

Meanwhile, anything inside the oven which doesn't contain moisture (a plate, for instance) is unaffected by the microwaves: they pass straight through it, like light through a pane of glass. That's why the dish containing the food doesn't get hot, although the heat from the food itself will warm the dish to a certain extent.

Microwave Oven Features

With so many different brands and models of microwave oven now on the market, there's also an ever-increasing number of different features to look out for. Here is a summary of the more useful ones.

Stirrers and Turntables

When the microwaves enter the oven, they are travelling more or less in straight lines. Cooking in this way would produce uneven results, because the food would absorb microwave energy from the same direction all the time.

To overcome the problem, the microwaves must be "distributed" evenly around the oven. Most manufacturers achieve this effect by incorporating either a Stirrer or a Turntable into the oven.

Stirrers

This device literally "stirs" the microwaves as they enter this oven, breaking up their straight lines and reflecting them more evenly around the cavity. The stirrer is usually situated in the oven ceiling, so it does not occupy useful cooking space.

Turntables

Many microwave ovens are equipped with an automatic turntable, which rotates the food through the microwaves in order to ensure that it is cooked evenly.

Memory Controls

Ovens with built-in memory controls can follow a multi-stage cooking cycle automatically — for instance, defrosting, roasting and then cooking. They can also be programmed in advance, like a video recorder, so that you can go out for the day and come home to find a cooked meal waiting for you.

Temperature Probe

This instrument has a needle-like point and is plugged into a socket inside the oven. The "needle" is inserted into the centre of the food and monitors the temperature during cooking. When the right temperature to complete the cooking process is reached, the probe switches the oven off automatically. It can be inserted through cling film or a roasting bag.

Convection Cooking

This method of cooking is similar to a conventional oven: hot air is circulated around the oven at a constant temperature so that the food is evenly cooked. Especially useful when baking scones, biscuits, bread etc, and also for roasting potatoes, chops and steaks.

Automatic Sensing

The "automatic sensing" facility found on some of today's more advanced microwave ovens is controlled by a microprocessor. As the food heats up and begins to give off steam, the microprocessor calculates the necessary cooking time by measuring the degree of humidity — rather like a barometer. The oven switches off automatically when the food is cooked, so you don't have to make your own timing calculations based on weight. Food cooked in this way should be completely wrapped in clingfilm (see "Note on Clingfilm", page 25), or cooked in a dome dish (see "Useful Accessories" page 18).

The oven door should not be opened during sensor cooking, because this could change the humidity/temperature conditions inside and spoil the end result.

The Combination Oven

A combination cooker is, quite simply, a marriage between two kinds of oven: a variable power microwave and an ordinary electric convection oven. This combination of two-cooking-systems-in-one-oven seeks to give you the best of both worlds: all the facilities of a conventional oven, plus the speed and cleanliness of a microwave.

Two cooking systems, of course, allow three ways of working: (1) microwave only, (2) convection only, or (3) a combination of the two. Some combination cookers contain a grill as well (exactly like a conventional grill) which can also be used in combination with microwave power.

Most combination cookers have turntables (to rotate the food during microwaving) and a built-in fan to assist the distribution of convection-generated hot air and to cool the oven between each cooking stage.

In other respects, features and specifications tend to vary a good deal. On some cookers, you must select both the convection oven temperature and the microwave power yourself. Others have their own weight-based Auto Sensor programmes for different categories of food. With these programmes, you enter the weight of the food on the oven's memory touch-pad, and it is then defrosted ("Auto-Weight Defrost") or cooked ("Auto-Weight Control") automatically.

All the variations among combination cookers make it essential to study the handbook/cookbook supplied with your model, and practise on the recipes it contains. When it comes to adapting your own recipes for combination cooking, a certain amount of trial and error will be necessary.

However, owners will find the effort worthwhile: combination cookers offer the possibility of speedily-cooked food with a crisp, traditional browned texture when you want it, yet with the freshness, flavour and nutritional goodness you expect from a microwave.

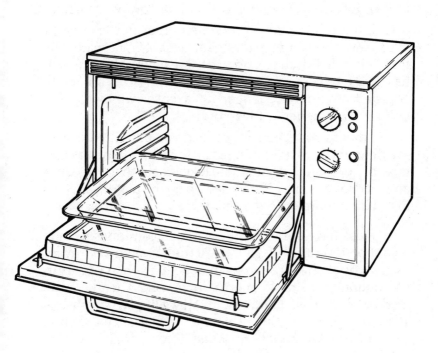

Cooking Time

How long you cook a particular item of food for is the 64,000-dollar question in successful microwave cooking.

One thing it depends on is the output power of your oven. The most common ratings are 600/650/700 watts; the times given in this book apply to those figures. If your oven has a different power rating, the cooking times have to adjusted accordingly; longer for a lower-wattage oven, shorter for a higher-wattage oven.

Another factor is how much food you put into the oven at a time, and how it is arranged on the plate. Two sausages take longer than one, and three take longer than two. And any food takes longer if it's piled up on the plate than if it's distributed more or less evenly.

You also have to remember that food continues to cook for a short time after you remove it from a microwave oven. That's why all the experts recommend that when you are in any doubt, you should aim to undercook. Then take the food out of the oven and test it. After all, you can always add a little cooking time if necessary; but once a dish is overcooked, it's too late to do anything about it. Fortunately, a microwave oven lets you interrupt the cooking process like this at any time without spoiling the food.

The only completely truthful answer to the question of timing is that you learn by experience. So start with the Introductory Dishes given on pages 34-55 of this book, to provide yourself with the basic grounding. Then go on to experimenting, introducing variations of your own and making a note of the results. That way, you'll be able to repeat your successes, correct your mistakes, and quickly gain the same familiarity with your microwave oven as you have with your ordinary cooker.

Meal Planning

Until you've mastered the basic techniques of microwave cooking, you'll probably find it difficult to cook a whole meal successfully by the new method. It's not so much the preparation of the food which changes as the speed at which it cooks — which means that the different stages of making a meal are sometimes undertaken in an unfamiliar order.

For instance, some parts of a meal can be cooked in advance, kept in the fridge and then heated up just before you're ready to eat. This applies particularly to vegetables, desserts, soups and sauces. Egg-and-cheese-based dishes, on the other hand, tend to cook very quickly and can therefore be overcooked by reheating: always cook these just before serving them.

Remember, too, that most food cooked by microwave must be given a period of standing time before being served. So you should start with the largest/slowest-cooking item (e.g. a joint), and cook the quicker items while it "stands". Anything which is too cool when it's time to be served can of course be given a few seconds in the microwave to bring it up to the right temperature.

Another useful tip is to make a habit of cooking more than you need, whether cooking by microwave or conventionally. The "left-over" food can then be covered and frozen for later use. In this way, you will build up a bank of ready-plated meals which can be defrosted and reheated in a matter of minutes for latecomers or unexpected guests — or on days when you yourself don't happen to feel like cooking!

Cooking Utensils

The most important rule about the utensils which go inside a microwave oven is; *if it's wholly or partly made of metal, don't use it*. Not because it's dangerous to you — it isn't — but because metal reflects microwaves away from the food and therefore slows down the cooking time in an irregular way. Prolonged use of metal utensils will also have a harmful effect on the oven.

Instead, use utensils made of glass (including Pyrex-type), pottery or china. These should have no metal handles or trim, and no metallic decoration, such as gold paint.

Rigid plastic utensils are all right (not flimsy plastic, like yoghurt pots), though these tend to get hotter to the touch and can be deformed by prolonged contact with hot food. Plastic or wooden spoons, bamboo skewers and wooden cocktail sticks can all be safely left inside the oven for short periods of time.

The shape of your cookware is also important: circular shapes like bowls, round dishes and ring moulds are ideal, and will produce the most even results. Food placed in square or rectangular dishes is liable to overcook at the corners.

If you don't own a ring mould, you can achieve the same effect by inverting a glass or jar in the middle of a round dish. Clingfilm (see "Note on Clingfilm", page 25) can be used to cover food during cooking, provided it is cut or punctured to allow a small amount of air to reach the food and prevent ballooning. Foil may also be used, in small quantities, but should not be allowed to touch any part of the oven itself. Prepared meals in foil trays should be transferred to another dish before cooking.   Roasting bags are also suitable: they should be pierced to allow steam to escape, and their metal ties must be replaced by elastic bands or string.

If In Doubt

If you are in any doubt as to whether a particular utensil is suitable or not, try the following test:

Put the utensil and half a glass of water into the oven side by side and heat on "High" for one minute. If the utensil is still cool to the touch, it may be used for microwave cooking, but not otherwise.

One extra tip: use oven gloves to remove dishes from the oven if they've been cooking for five minutes or more. The microwaves won't heat the container, but the hot food will.

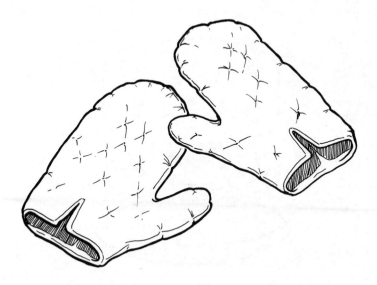

Useful Accessories

Specialist microwave shops offer a variety of accessories and cookware to help you adapt to cooking by microwave. In this section I have listed the ones which I find most useful.

Dome Dish Set

This compact and useful set consists of three dishes: the tray (with a lip, for pouring); a roasting rack, which fits inside the tray; and a transparent, domed cover. Useful for cooking joints of meat, and also stews, casseroles etc, since the dome can be inverted for use as a saucepan, with the tray acting as the lid.

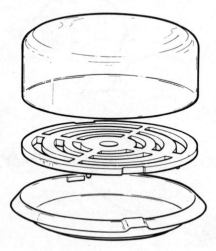

Microwave Plastic Ware

Generally made of a strong plastic, and sold in packs of three or four. Very inexpensive, but long-lasting and serviceable, in a variety of useful shapes and sizes. Also suitable for freezing.
WARNING: Not to be used with Browning Dish or in Browning Oven.

Plate Stacking Rings

Sturdy plastic rings used to stack already-plated meals for reheating in the microwave oven.

Roasting Rack

When a joint is cooked on a roasting rack, the juices are drained off the meat and the final result is more even. The rack is also useful for cooking bacon to a brown and crispy finish, and for sausages, burgers etc.

Muffin Pan

May be used for poaching eggs, making individual cakes and pies, mini Xmas puddings etc. Cooks 6 at a time.

Pyrex-type Jugs

Available in various sizes. Useful for making custard, scrambled eggs, sauces etc. as the food remains completely visible during cooking - a big advantage when preparing milk-based recipes which tend to boil very rapidly in a microwave oven.

Soufflé Dishes (6", 7" or 8")

Excellent substitute for cake tins. Available in ceramic or Pyrex.

Oval Pie Dishes

Check that the dishes will turn without obstruction on your turntable before purchase. Use for egg custards, milk puddings, cottage pie etc. Available in ceramic or Pyrex.

Other Utensils

Since metal utensils are not suitable for microwave use, the following are recommended:
Plastic/Wooden Spatula
Wooden Spoon.

Variable Power

This facility allows you, in effect, to vary your oven's cooking temperature just as you can with your ordinary cooker. Many foods can be cooked perfectly on a single setting, but others require two or more settings to achieve the best results. For example, a joint of meat should be cooked at a very high temperature for a short time, to seal in the juices, and then finished more slowly, at a lower setting.

Variable power works by pulsing microwaves into the oven in a series of on/off cycles. Each setting on your oven's control knob operates a different cycle: the higher the setting, the more time the microwaves are "on" within the cycle. This variation simulates temperature change and allows food to be cooked at different speeds.

When learning to use variable power, it's a good idea to base your timing calculations on the weight of the food. However, the guide set out below is only approximate, since different foods cook at different speeds: density, moisture content and starting temperature are just 3 of the variable factors.

Variable Power Settings *(applicable to 600/650 watt ovens)*
High: 8 mins. per lb.
Roast: 10-11 mins. per lb.
Simmer: 12-14 mins. per lb.
Defrost: 8 mins. per lb.
Stew: 20-22 mins. per lb.
Warm: Only used for keeping food hot.

When cooking food in a 2-stage process (starting on the "High" setting), allow approximately 1 minute per lb of the total weight.

EXAMPLE: Roasting a 3 lb joint.
Stage 1: 1 min. per lb on "High" = 3 minutes
Stage 2: 10 mins. per lb on "Roast" = 30 minutes

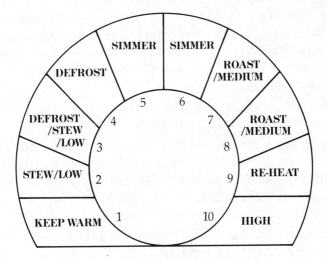

The cooking modes which a microwave oven can perform are shown on its control panel. The simplest ovens have only 2 or 3 possible settings (e.g. HIGH, MEDIUM and LOW), while more sophisticated models have dials or touch control panels marked with either numbers (1,2,3,4 etc) or words (e.g. ROAST, SIMMER, STEW, etc). The diagram above illustrates how these different ways of displaying the cooking modes relate to each other.

For a precise explanation of the settings on your own oven, refer to the handbook supplied by the manufacturer.

Defrosting

This is one of the most useful and convenient facilities which a microwave oven provides. Not only can food be defrosted in a matter of minutes, but more of its natural juices are retained as well. There is also no accumulation of bacteria, as there is with conventional thawing.

For microwave beginners, the secret of successful defrosting is in the weighing of the food. As an approximate guide, allow 7-8 minutes defrost time to every 1 lb of food. Always give the food a further 8-12 minutes rest period after defrosting and before starting to cook, in order to make sure that the defrosting process is complete. Wrappings should be loosened and metal ties removed before defrosting.

But how do you thaw out frozen food in a microwave oven without also starting to cook it?

The basic answer is that the microwaves must be released in an on/off/on/off cycle. ON for a few seconds, or minutes, to start the thawing, then OFF for a rest period, to ensure that the cooking process does not start at this stage. Then ON again, OFF again, and so on.

If your oven has a DEFROST setting, this procedure is performed automatically. If not, you have to do it by hand. Exactly how long the ON and OFF cycles should be depends on what you are thawing; the smaller the item, the less time it takes. Small items like fishcakes and beefburgers can be cooked without any defrosting; this is indicated, where appropriate, in the Introductory Dishes section beginning on page 34 of this book.

Reheating

Your microwave oven is ideal for reheating pre-cooked food — not only because it's so quick, but also because the food won't dry out, losing colour and flavour, as in an ordinary oven.

Arrange the food evenly around the dish/plate, with larger items towards the edge, and cover with a lid or cling film during reheating. Use plate stacking rings for reheating more than one plateful at the same time.

When you are reheating several items together, arrange them in a circle inside the oven with the centre preferably left empty. The "ring" arrangement is the ideal pattern for microwave cooking.

Remember that any dishes containing plenty of liquid (casseroles, soups, sauces etc.) should be stirred during and after reheating.

Note on Clingfilm

Evidence has been found that small quantities of plasticiser (a chemical used to make PVC clingfilm flexible) can "migrate" into some food if the film and the food are in contact during microwave cooking. Government research indicates that the danger to health is minimal, but if you are worried, you can use polyethylene film (which contains no plasticiser) instead of PVC film. Look at the package before you buy: if the film contains no plasticiser, that fact will be stated on the box, or label.

Browning

One thing that microwaves won't do on their own is to turn food brown in the way an ordinary oven does. The reason is that the microwaves themselves are not hot; the heat is generated *within* the food, not applied from the outside.

This problem, however, is quite easily solved. There are three principal methods.

Colouring

In this case, the brown colour is achieved simply by rubbing gravy browning, or a brown-coloured spice such as paprika, onto the surface of the food before cooking. This method is commonly used when roasting a chicken, for instance.

Other useful ingredients for colouring include soy sauce and Worcester sauce (for savoury dishes), an egg-and-milk glaze (for pastry) and brown sugar, treacle and wholemeal flour (for cakes etc).

Browning Element/Hot Air Convector

Some microwave ovens have a browning element built into their ceiling. It works rather like an electric grill, and browns food either before or during cooking.

Other ovens feature a convected hot air system as well as microwaves, which permits them to brown food in the same way as a conventional oven. Obviously, these methods are only applicable to those with suitable ovens (see page 12-13).

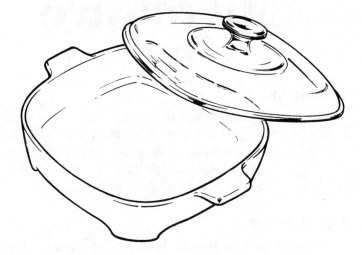

The Browning Dish

This useful accessory can be used in any microwave oven. It is specially made of a combination glass/ceramic substance with a metal oxide coating which becomes hot when exposed to microwaves. The empty dish is brushed with oil and heated in the oven. The food is then placed on it to brown, and turned to brown the other sides. How long you heat the browning dish for, and how long you leave the food in it, depends on what you are cooking; if in doubt, refer to the manufacturers' instructions.

Aluminium browning dishes are also available, usually in the form of a skillet with a non-stick surface. These are used in the same way as ceramic browning dishes.

Some practical examples of browning dish use are given on page 50. Always make sure you wear oven gloves when removing the browning dish from the oven after use.

You can help a joint of meat or poultry to brown by cooking it in a roast bag. Remember to pierce the bag and replace any metal ties by elastic bands or string.

Care of Your Microwave Oven

Installation

Your microwave oven can be installed in the kitchen, bedroom, or any other place where there's a fused 13 amp or 15 amp socket. A worktop or strong shelf provides suitable support, or the oven can be built in provided that you leave adequate space around the air vents.

Maintenance

Microwave ovens are easy to look after, and a few simple rules help to maintain them in good working order.

— Make sure that there is no obstruction when you close the oven door, or the door seal could be damaged.

— Keep a glass of water in the oven when it is not being used. Accidentally operating the oven with nothing inside can damage the magnetron.

— Have the oven examined every year or so to check that its performance is correct. Repairs and servicing should only be carried out by qualified personnel.

Safety

Microwave ovens are manufactured in accordance with statutory safety regulations and standards. Leakage is in any case prevented by special seals, and locks on the oven door which stop microwave generation as soon as the door is opened.

Cleaning

It's important to keep your oven clean, because old spills will absorb microwaves and reduce the oven's efficiency. Fortunately any food which spills does not bake where it falls, as in a conventional oven, so it's easy to remove. Just wipe the inside surfaces of the oven with a damp cloth after each use, and keep the door seal free from accumulated grease or food. If a spill is hard to remove, boil a container of water in the oven for a few minutes — the steam will loosen it. Do not use abrasives or other chemical cleaners.

Converting Your own Recipes

A large proportion of the recipes you cook in your ordinary oven can be successfully adapted for cooking by microwave. (Exceptions include eggs in the shell, some types of pastry and Yorkshire pudding.) Many of the basic preparation and cooking techniques apply to both methods;the main difference is the timing.

Unfortunately, accurate instructions on making the conversion are impossible to give because of the variation in each person's recipes and type of microwave oven. Once again, experience is the only reliable way to learn. The following points should be remembered:

— Since microwaves act on moisture, recipes which involve cooking in liquid (boiling/steaming/casseroling etc) are easiest to convert.

— The "microwave version" of your recipe will require approx. 25% less liquid than usual. More can be added during cooking if necessary.

— Use larger cookware than usual, to avoid boiling over.

— Mixtures which rise during cooking (e.g. cakes) should not occupy more than $\frac{1}{2}$ the dish before cooking begins.

— Always underestimate the cooking time required and check the food frequently during cooking.

— Always allow for a short period of "standing time" during which the cooking process will be completed.

Useful Tips

1 When cooking meat or vegetables, always cover the dish. This helps the food to cook more quickly, and prevents drying out.

2 When using a Browning Dish, always brush with oil *before* heating. Adding oil after the dish is heated slows the cooking time.

3 When cooking a milk-based recipe (e.g. rice pudding), use a dish at least twice as large as the amount of food being cooked. This allows for the tendency of milk to boil over suddenly.

4 Salt added to uncooked food should always be dissolved first in a little water. Sprinkling salt directly tends to toughen and dehydrate the food.

5 Cooking for holidays (Christmas, Easter, etc): all vegetables can be cooked in advance and frozen, so they only need reheating on the day.

6 Heavy coffee drinkers: make a jug of coffee and keep it in the fridge, warming up cupfuls as required.

7 Freezer owners: build a "bank" of prepared meals by cooking more than you need and freezing the remainder. Useful for unexpected guests and, particularly, for youngsters, who can heat their own meal without difficulty or danger.

8 To save washing up:
(i) Line the dish with greaseproof paper when baking a cake.
(ii) Heat soups, cereals etc in the dishes out of which you plan to eat.

9 To sterilize baby bottles, or jam jars: wash and shake the bottle/jar then heat for 5 minutes on HIGH, or until dry.

10 A dish with no lid can always be covered by a dinner plate. The plate will then be warmed, ready for serving.

11 To soften butter: warm the pack on DEFROST for 30 seconds.

12 If you do not have a roasting rack, use two upturned saucers side by side instead.

13 To "freshen" bread rolls, jam doughnuts etc: heat on HIGH for 10-20 seconds each.

14 The use of brown sugar will make all the difference to the colour of dessert foods — especially cakes.

15 To melt gelatine: break into a bowl with 4 tblspns of water and heat on DEFROST for 2 minutes.

16 To dry damp salt or sugar: heat on HIGH for 20-30 seconds.

17 To get the maximum juice from oranges/lemons: heat on HIGH for 10 seconds (not more) before squeezing.

18 To remove tomato skins easily: prick skins and heat on HIGH for 1 minute (4 tomatoes)

19 To peel chestnuts:make 2 cuts in each chestnut (to prevent bursting) and heat on HIGH for 1 minute (8 oz).

20 To dry herbs: lay between two sheets of kitchen paper and heat on HIGH for 25 seconds (or until dry). Allow to stand before packing.

21 To flavour cake icing: grate rind from an orange or lemon, place in a saucer and heat on HIGH for 30 seconds. Add to caster sugar when making cake icing.

22 Quick chocolate cake topping: break 4 oz. chocolate bar into a dish and heat on HIGH for 2 minutes. Remove, stir and spread.

23 To make breadcrumbs: take 1 slice of bread and heat on HIGH for 2 minutes or until dry. Wrap in cloth and crush.

24 When cooking fish: brush with oil/melted butter to prevent drying out.

25 To rehydrate fruit: put 8 oz. dried fruit in a dish and just cover with water. Heat on HIGH for 5 minutes.

PART 2

Introductory Dishes

HOT DRINKS
MEAT
FISH
VEGETABLES
PUDDINGS
MISCELLANEOUS
THE BROWNING DISH
CONVENIENCE FOODS

IMPORTANT NOTE

1. Microwave cookbooks cannot give exact cooking times for particular foods because of variations in the type of oven being used, the starting temperature and density of the food, and different individuals' personal preferences.

Throughout this book, cooking times are recommended thus:

E.g. 5-6 (or 5-6-7) minutes on HIGH.
700 watt ovens — use shortest time given.
650 watt ovens — use the middle figure (or average).
600 watt ovens — use the longest time given.

2. Reheat times: always use HIGH setting.

HOT DRINKS

ITEM	PREPARATION	SETTING
INSTANT COFFEE	Mix coffee, milk and water in cup or jug	High
HOT MILK	Pour milk into jug or cup	High
TEA	Put water in ceramic jug or pot	High
DRINKING CHOCOLATE	Mix drinking chocolate and milk in mug or cup ($\frac{3}{4}$ full)	High
MALTED MILK	Stir malted milk mix together with milk in a mug or cup ($\frac{3}{4}$ full)	High

COOKING TIME	REMARKS	REHEAT TIME
2-2½-3 min per pint	Add sugar *after* heating the coffee	
2-2½-3 min per ½ pint (2½ min per cup)	Use large cooking vessel to prevent spillage	
4-5-6 min per ½ pint	Make tea as usual	
2-2½-3 min per ½ pint	Stir after 1 minute	
2-2½-3 min per ½ pint	Stir after 1 minute	

MEAT

ITEM	PREPARATION	SETTING
BACON RASHERS	Place on rack between two paper plates (one acting as a lid), or between two sheets of kitchen paper.	High
BEEF BURGERS	Place between two ceramic plates (one acting as lid)	High
MINCED BEEF	Crumble into dish with tight-fitting lid	High
CHICKEN PORTIONS (2)	Brush with margarine or butter, rub in paprika and/or seasoning if required. Enclose dish in roast bag and place on rack.	High
GRAVY	Mix gravy powder and stock to normal consistency. Place in dish and stir.	High

COOKING TIME	REMARKS	REHEAT TIME
45 secs-1 min per rasher		
45 secs-1 min per burger		
5-6-8 min	Cover dish during cooking	2-3 min per portion
12 min (6-7 min per portion) approx.	Defrosting: 3 min per portion	1 min per portion
2-4 min	Stir every 30 sec. Cook until thickened	1-2 min

FISH

ITEM	PREPARATION	SETTING
COD HADDOCK (STEAMED)	Dot fish with butter and lay between two plates *(one acting as lid)*	High
KIPPERS (FROZEN)	Dot kippers with butter and lay between two plates *(one acting as lid)*	High
TROUT	Garnish with almond, butter and seasoning to taste.	High
FISH FINGERS	Lay between 2 plates *(one acting as lid)*	High
FISH CAKES	Lay between 2 plates *(one acting as lid)*	High

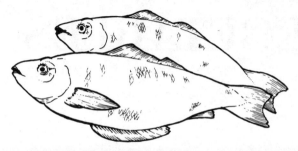

COOKING TIME	REMARKS	REHEAT TIME
2-3 min (½lb) 5-6 min (1lb)	Defrost before cooking: 7 min per lb	3-4 min per portion
1 min per kipper approx	No need to defrost in advance	30-45 secs. per portion
5-6-7 min per lb	Cover during cooking	
30 secs each *(fresh)* 45 secs each *(frozen)*	No need to defrost in advance. See also "Browning Dish"	
20 secs each *(fresh)* 30 secs each *(frozen)*	No need to defrost in advance. See also "Browning Dish"	

VEGETABLES

ITEM	PREPARATION	SETTING
BRUSSELS SPROUTS	Trim and split stalk-ends. Place in $\frac{1}{2}''$ water in a dish.	High
CABBAGE	Shred into medium sized pieces. Place in $\frac{1}{2}''$ water in a dish.	High
CARROTS PARSNIPS SWEDES TURNIPS	Peel and slice. Place in $\frac{1}{2}''$ water in a dish.	High
CAULIFLOWER	Cut into florets. Shred leafstalks if required. Place in $\frac{1}{2}$-$\frac{3}{4}''$ of water in a dish.	High
CORN ON THE COB	Brush with butter and place on plate.	High
MUSHROOMS	Wash, peel and slice *(or prepare as required)*. Place in dish with seasoning, knob of butter and 1 tablespoon water.	High

COOKING TIME	REMARKS	REHEAT TIME
7-8-9 min (1 lb) 13-14 min (2 lb)	Cover during cooking	3-4 min per lb
7-8-10 min (1 lb)	Cover during cooking. Turn the cabbage over after 5 min	3-4 min per lb
9-10-12 min (1 lb) 16-18- 20 min (2 lb)	Cover during cooking	3-4 min per lb
7-8-10 min (1 lb) 13-15- 16 min (2 lb)	Cover during cooking. Turn cauliflower over after 5 min	3-4 min per lb
3-4 min per cob *(fresh)* 4-5 min per cob *(frozen)*	No need to defrost in advance. Fresh cobs should be wrapped in cling film *(pierced)*	1 min per cob
2-3 min ($\frac{1}{4}$ lb) 3-4 min ($\frac{1}{2}$ lb)	Cover during cooking	1 min per serving

ITEM	PREPARATION	SETTING
ONIONS	Chop and season onions. Place in $\frac{1}{4}''$ water in a dish	High
PEAS (FRESH)	Shell and place in $\frac{1}{2}$-$\frac{3}{4}''$ water in a dish	High
PEAS (FROZEN)	For $\frac{1}{2}$ lb or less, place in a dish without water. For amounts over $\frac{1}{2}$ lb, add $\frac{1}{2}$-$\frac{3}{4}''$ water.	High
POTATOES (BOILED)	Peel potatoes. Place in $\frac{1}{2}''$ of salted water in a dish.	High
POTATOES (JACKET)	Wash and pierce potatoes (to prevent splitting)	High
RUNNER BEANS (FRESH)	Place in $\frac{1}{2}$-$\frac{3}{4}''$ water in a dish.	High
RUNNER BEANS (FROZEN)	Place in $\frac{1}{2}$-$\frac{3}{4}''$ water in a dish.	High
TOMATOES (2)	Cut in half and place on plate.	High

COOKING TIME	REMARKS	REHEAT TIME
2-3 min per medium onion	Cover during cooking	
6-7 min (1 lb) 10-11 min (2 lb)	Cover during cooking	3 min per lb
6-7 min (1lb) 10-11 min (2lb)	Cover during cooking. No need to defrost in advance	3 min per lb
10-12 min (1 lb) 16-18- 20 min (2 lb)	Cover during cooking	5-6 min
5-6 min (1 med potato) 16-18 min (4 med potatoes)	Lay on kitchen paper to cook.	1 min per potato
8-10-12 min (1 lb) 15-16- 18 min (2 lb)	Cover during cooking	3 min per lb
7-8 min ($\frac{1}{2}$ lb) 13-14 min (1 lb)	Cover during cooking. No need to defrost in advance.	3 min per lb
30-45sec. each		

PUDDINGS

ITEM	PREPARATION	SETTING
APPLES (BAKED)	Core the apples. Score skins and fill centres with brown sugar and raisins. Place on a dish.	High
APPLES (STEWED)	Peel, core and slice apples. Place in $\frac{1}{2}''$ water in a dish. Sprinkle with sugar.	High
CUSTARD	Follow preparation instructions on tin. Mix thoroughly, then place in a large Pyrex-type jar.	High
QUICK MERINGUE	Mix 10 oz. icing sugar with 1 egg white, in a fondant. Divide mixture into marble-sized pieces. Cook 4 at a time on greaseproof paper.	High
SHORTCAKE	Mix 6 oz. plain flour with 2 oz. castor sugar. Add 4 oz. margarine, rub in thoroughly. Press the mixture into a greased 7" flan dish.	High
SHORTCAKE TOPPING	Break 1 Mars bar into a dish and melt.	High

COOKING TIME	REMARKS	REHEAT TIME
3 min (1 apple) 5 min (2 apples) 8 min (4 apples)		1 min per apple
5-6 min (1lb apples)	Cover during cooking	2 min per portion
5-6 min per pint approx.	Use large enough cooking vessel to allow room for custard to boil up. Stir once during cooking.	3 min per pint $1\frac{1}{2}$-2 min per $\frac{1}{2}$ pint
40 secs – 1 min per batch of 4	After cooking, sandwich together with fresh whipped cream and serve.	
$2\frac{1}{2}$-3 min	Allow to cool and mark into wedges.	
1 min	Allow to cool slightly before pouring onto shortcake.	

MISCELLANEOUS

ITEM	PREPARATION	SETTING
PIZZA (READY-COOKED)	Place on a plate	High
PORRIDGE	Mix porridge with milk, water, salt or sugar *(to taste)* in a cereal bowl. Stir.	High
RICE (PATNA-TYPE)	Put $\frac{1}{2}$ pint water in a dish and heat. —— THEN ——	High
	Add 4oz rice with seasoning *(serves 2)*	High
EGG (POACHED)	Put 2 tablespoonfuls water in a teacup, and heat. —— THEN ——	High
	Add the egg	High
EGG (SCRAMBLED)	Mix eggs, butter, milk, salt, pepper in Pyrex-type jug. Heat mixture. —— THEN ——	High
	Stir mixture once and continue cooking	High

COOKING TIME	REMARKS	REHEAT TIME
1 min *(fresh)* 2 min *(frozen)*	No need to defrost in advance	
2-3 min per portion	Stir porridge halfway through cooking	1 min per portion
7 min		3 min per portion
8 min	Cook until water is absorbed.	
30 sec		
30 sec	Use one teacup for each egg	
30 sec		
1 min, or until egg mixture rises and thickens.	Watch cooking in progress. Eggs rise up when ready.	

THE BROWNING DISH

ITEM	Browning Dish Preheat Time (on "High")	PREPARATION
BEEF BURGERS	6-7 min (with $\frac{1}{2}$ tblspn oil)	Place beefburger in the dish.
BACON	6-7 min (with 1 tblspn oil)	Place bacon in the dish
SAUSAGES	8 min (with 1 tblspn oil)	Place sausages in the dish
CHOPS	9 min (with $\frac{1}{2}$ tblspn oil)	Place chops in the dish.
JOINT OF MEAT (TO SEAR AND SEAL)	9 min (with 1 tblspn oil)	Roll joint in the hot fat, sealing on all sides.

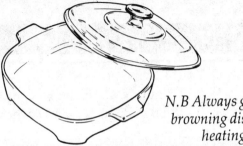

N.B Always grease the browning dish before heating it.

SETTING	COOKING TIME	REMARKS
High	30 sec each *(1 min if frozen)*	Turn over halfway through cooking
High	20 sec each side of each rasher	
High	2 min per sausage	Turn over half way through cooking.
High	6-7 min per lb	Turn over halfway through cooking.
High		

ITEM	Browning Dish Preheat Time (on "High")	PREPARATION
EGGS (FRIED)	4 min (with oil in dish)	Break eggs into dish and cover with lid
4-EGG OMELETTE	$3\frac{1}{2}$ min (with $\frac{1}{2}$ tblspn oil)	Tip beaten omelette mixture into dish.Cover with lid.
CHIPS	8 min ($\frac{1}{2}''$ of oil in the dish)	Make the chips from parboiled potatoes.
FISH CAKES **FISH FINGERS**	6-7 min (with $\frac{1}{2}$ tblspn oil)	Place fish fingers/ cakes in the dish.
BREADED FISH	5-6 min (with 2 tblspn oil)	Place fish in dish
WHITEBAIT	5-6 min (with $\frac{1}{2}$ tblspn oil)	Place whitebait in dish
STEAK	6-7min (no oil)	Add teaspoon of butter. Lay steak in dish.

SETTING	COOKING TIME	REMARKS
High	15 sec per egg	
High	2-3 min	Turn out with spatula
High	2-3 min per $\frac{1}{2}$ lb	Turn over halfway through cooking
High	30 sec each *(fresh)* 45 sec *(frozen)*	Turn over half way through cooking.
High	5-6 min per lb	Turn over halfway through cooking
High	5-6 min per lb	Turn over halfway through cooking
High	3 min per lb *(rare)* $4\frac{1}{2}$ min per lb *(medium)* 6-7 min per lb *(well done)*	

CONVENIENCE FOODS

ITEM	SETTING	COOKING TIME
PREPARED MEALS	High	3-4 min per portion *(fresh)* 6-7 min per portion *(frozen)*
SOUP (TINNED)	Med	2-3 min per portion
BAKED BEANS	High	1-1$\frac{1}{2}$ min per portion *(cover while cooking)*
SPAGHETTI (TINNED)	High	1-1$\frac{1}{2}$ min per portion *(cover while cooking)*

ITEM	SETTING	COOKING TIME
MEAT PIES/PASTIES	High	1 min per pie *(1½ min if frozen)*. Pierce crust with knife before cooking.
PUDDINGS (TINNED)	High	1-2 min per portion
FRUIT PIES/TARTS	High	1-1½ min *(individual size)* 2-3 min *(family size)*
BREAKFAST CEREALS (WITH MILK)	High	1 min per portion

PART 3

*Everyday
Microwave
Recipes*

Beef Stew

$\frac{3}{4}$ lb. beef, cubed

2 large carrots

$\frac{1}{2}$ small swede

1 large parsnip

$\frac{1}{2}$ lb. leeks

1 small onion

3 medium potatoes

1 pint beef stock

Seasoning

Chop the vegetables.

Place all the ingredients in a large dish with a lid.

Cook for 10 minutes on HIGH.

Remove from oven and stir.

Cook for 70 minutes on LOW, stirring 3 or 4 times during cooking.

Liver and Bacon Savoury

1 lb. liver
6 rashers bacon
$\frac{1}{4}$ lb. mixed stuffing
Seasoning to taste

Pierce the liver several times with a fork.

Place liver in the dish, cover with stuffing and lay bacon rashers on top.

Cook for 25 minutes on MEDIUM.

Bacon Rolls

8 oz. sage and onion stuffing (for preparation, see page 81).

8 rashers streaky bacon

Wooden cocktail sticks

Divide stuffing into 8 portions.

Wrap a bacon rasher around each portion and hold in place with a cocktail stick.

Place the bacon rolls on a roasting rack.

Cook for 8-10 minutes on HIGH.

Spare Ribs

Serves 4

Ribs: 8-10 spare ribs
Sauce:
1 medium onion, finely chopped
1 dessertspoon cooking oil
4 oz. tomato puree
3 tablespoons dry mustard
3 oz. brown sugar
2 teaspoons lemon juice
2 tablespoons brown sauce
1 tablespoon cornflour

Place all the sauce ingredients in a liquidiser and blend until smooth.

Arrange the ribs in a shallow dish. Cook *(uncovered)* for 5 minutes on HIGH.

Drain off surplus fat.

Pour liquidised sauce over the ribs.

Cook for 5 minutes on HIGH, then for 15-20 minutes on ROAST.

Chili Con Carne

1 lb. minced beef
1 beef stock cube
1 med. can tomatoes (roughly chopped)
Small tin red kidney beans (drained)
1 packet chili con carne mix OR
$1\frac{1}{2}$ level dessertspoons chili powder

Cook minced beef for 4-5 minutes on HIGH.

Drain off fat.

Crumble in stock cube and add all other ingredients.

Cook for 5-8 minutes on HIGH.

NB: Stir halfway through cooking.

Cottage Pie

1 lb. minced beef
1 medium onion, diced
¼ pint stock
1 lb. potatoes, mashed and seasoned

Cook meat and onion together *(uncovered)* for 4-5 minutes on HIGH.

Drain off fat and add the stock.

Cook *(covered)* for 4-5 minutes on HIGH.

Remove and top with mashed potatoes.

Cook for 2-3 minutes on HIGH.

Pork Chops in Sweet 'n' Sour Sauce

4 chops
1 medium onion (chopped)
1 small can tomatoes (roughly chopped)
1 teaspoon Worcester sauce
1 teaspoon sweet pickle
1 dessertspoon lemon juice
1 tablespoon demerara sugar
Seasoning to taste
1 tablespoon oil (for frying)

Brush browning dish with oil and preheat for 6-7 minutes on HIGH.

Cook chops in browning dish for 6-7 minutes per lb. *(less if the bone content is high).*

Turn chops over once during cooking.

Remove from dish.

Place chopped onion into browning dish. Cook *(covered)* for 2-3 minutes on HIGH.

Add all the other ingredients and stir.

Cook for 2 minutes on HIGH.

Pour sauce over chops and serve.

Savoury Minced Beef

1 lb. minced beef
14 oz. can tomatoes
1 chopped onion
$\frac{1}{2}$ lb. mixed vegetables (frozen or fresh diced).
$\frac{1}{4}$ pint beef stock

Cook mince and onions *(uncovered)* for 5 minutes on HIGH.

Drain off surplus fat.

Add other ingredients and mix thoroughly.

Cook mixture *(covered)* for 12-15 minutes on HIGH.

(Alternatively, cook for 30 minutes on SIMMER).

Beef Curry

1½ lbs. beef, cubed
1 medium onion, sliced
¼ pint beef stock
¼ pint tomato juice
¼ teaspoon salt
3 teaspoons curry powder
1 teaspoon lemon juice
2 tablespoons cooking oil

Place meat and onion in a large dish with a lid.
Cook for 8-10 minutes on HIGH.

Remove from oven, drain off fat and add remaining ingredients. Stir thoroughly.

Cook for 1 hr. 25 minutes on MEDIUM.

Chicken & Vegetable Curry

$\frac{1}{2}$ chicken - cooked and chopped

$\frac{1}{4}$ lb. mixed vegetables (chopped)

1 large onion (chopped)

$\frac{1}{2}$ cooking apple (chopped)

1 oz. butter

$\frac{1}{2}$ pint chicken stock

2 dessertspoons tomato purée

2 dessertspoons curry powder

2 dessertspoons cornflour

1 dessertspoon chutney

Stir the cornflour, chutney, tomato purée and curry powder to a smooth paste.

Gradually stir in the stock.

Cook the chopped onion with the butter *(covered)* for 4-5 minutes on HIGH.

Place all the ingredients in a dish, cover and cook for 10-11 minutes on HIGH.

Chicken & Vegetable Soup

Serves 4

½ chicken (or 1 large portion)
1 small turnip
1 small swede
1 medium parsnip
1 leek
1 medium onion
2 carrots
Knob of butter
1 chicken stock cube
¼ pint water
Seasoning to taste
Level tablespoon cornflour

Roughly chop all the vegetables.

Dissolve the stock cube in water.

Place all ingredients (except the cornflour) in a large dish (the chicken should be covered by the vegetables and the liquid).

Cook for 14-15 minutes on HIGH, then for 30 minutes on SIMMER.

Mix the cornflour with some stock. Add to soup.

Cook for 2-3 minutes on HIGH.

Stir, remove chicken bones and serve.

Corn Fritters

(using Browning Dish)

4 tablespoons cooking oil
2 tablespoons milk
4 oz. self-raising flour
$\frac{1}{2}$ level tspn mustard powder
2 eggs, beaten
4 oz. sweetcorn

Put the oil into the browning dish and heat for 5-6 minutes on HIGH.

Mix all the other ingredients together to form a batter.

Divide batter into spoonful-size portions and cook (3 at a time) for 2 minutes on HIGH.

Turn over once during cooking.

Pizza

Base:
       8 oz. plain flour
       3 oz. margarine
       Milk to mix
       1 tablespoon mixed herbs

Rub margarine into the flour and herbs.

Mix to a stiff dough with milk.

Preheat the browning dish for 5-6 minutes, brushing lightly with margarine when hot.

Roll out the dough.

Cook in the browning dish for 4-5 minutes on HIGH.

Topping:
       Tomato puree (to taste)
       4 rashers bacon (chopped)
       1 medium onion (chopped)
       2 oz. grated cheese
       Knob of butter

Add bacon to onion and butter.

Cover and cook for 4 minutes on HIGH.

Spread tomato purée over cooked base.

Place cooked bacon/onion mixture on top, then sprinkle with grated cheese. Cook for 2-3 minutes on HIGH, or until cheese has melted.

Sprinkle with paprika before serving.

Garlic Bread

2 oz. butter
1 clove garlic, crushed
Chopped parsley
Pinch of salt
1 French loaf

Blend the butter, salt, garlic and parsley together.

Cut the bread into slices, keeping the crust intact along the bottom of the loaf.

Spread the slices generously with the garlic butter mixture.

Wrap the loaf in greaseproof or kitchen paper and heat for 45 seconds — 1 minute on HIGH.

Steak & Kidney Pudding

Serves 4

1 lb. of steak and kidney
¾ pint stock, with salt added

Cook on HIGH for 4 minutes.
Then cook on LOW for 1 hour.
(More time may be necessary to tenderise the meat).

Pastry

6 oz. flour
3 oz. suet
Water to mix

Mix together to make a stiff dough.
Roll out, and line a 2 lb. pudding basin (greased), leaving enough dough for the top.
Fill with cooked steak and kidney.
Dampen the top edge of the dough and seal on the lid.
Cover with clingfilm and slit the top.
Cook on HIGH for 5-6 minutes.

Spaghetti Bolognese

Serves 4

Bolognese:

Small tin tomatoes
1 lb. minced beef
1 stock cube (beef)
1 onion (finely chopped)
Seasoning to taste

Cook beef and onions *(uncovered)* for 5-6 minutes on HIGH.

Drain off fat, add remaining ingredients.

Cook *(covered)* for 8-10 minutes on HIGH.

Spaghetti:

4 oz. spaghetti
1 pint boiling salted water

Put water into dish and gently lower in the spaghetti.

Cook for 10 minutes on HIGH.

Cover and leave to stand for 5 minutes.

Drain and serve.

Macaroni Cheese

Serves 2-3

8 oz. macaroni
Salt
1 teaspoon oil
1¾ pints boiling water

Combine these ingredients in a large dish.
Cook on HIGH 6-7 minutes.

1 oz. butter
1 oz. flour
1 pint milk
Seasoning to taste
6 oz. grated cheese

Heat the butter in a large *(fireproof)* dish for 1 minute on HIGH.

Blend in the flour. Cook for 30 seconds on HIGH.

Gradually blend in the milk. Cook for 3 minutes on HIGH, stirring every 1 minute.

Stir in the cheese.

Drain off macaroni, cover with cheese sauce, decorate by sprinkling paprika, and serve.

Savoury Quiche

Pastry: **6 oz. plain flour**

3 oz. margarine

Water to mix

1 egg yolk (beaten)

Make up pastry and use to line 8″ flan dish.
Prick all over with fork. Brush with egg yolk to
seal.   Cook for 3-4 minutes on HIGH.

Filling: **4 oz. grated cheese**

2 eggs

3 rashers bacon (chopped)

$\frac{1}{2}$ onion (chopped)

2 oz. mushrooms (chopped)

$\frac{1}{4}$ pint milk

1 oz. butter

Seasoning

Cook bacon, onion and butter together *(covered)*
for 3-4 minutes on HIGH.

Whisk eggs and milk with seasoning.

Add bacon and onion mixture to cooked flan case.

Cover with egg mixture. Sprinkle with cheese.

Cook for 10-11-12 minutes on HIGH.

Sprinkle with paprika before serving *(optional)*.

Roast Chicken

Wash and dry the chicken thoroughly, inside and out.

Stuff in the usual way if desired.

Brush with melted margarine/butter and sprinkle with paprika.

Cook on HIGH for 7-8-9 minutes per lb.

NB. Always use a roasting rack. Either cover the chicken with a lid or enclose it in a roasting bag sealed with an elastic band. Pierce the bottom of the bag to allow juices to escape. Some roasting racks do not have facilities for catching the excess fat, but a suitable container for this purpose is essential.

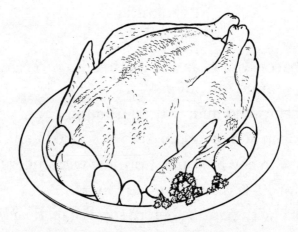

Roast Beef

Place the beef on a roasting rack and cover.

Cook in 2 stages:

a) on HIGH for 1 minute per lb.

b) on MEDIUM for 10-12 minutes per lb. (or 8-9 minutes per lb. for rare beef).

NB. Using a roasting bag will improve the colour of the joint. Make holes in the bottom, where it touches the rack, to allow juices to escape. Some roasting racks do not have facilities for catching the excess fat, but a suitable container for this purpose is essential.
Salt may be rubbed into the FAT only to improve crispness.

Roast Pork

Weigh the joint, score the skin, wash and pat dry.

Rub salt into the FAT only.

Place the joint in a roasting bag, sealing the end with an elastic band.

Pierce holes in the bag at the base.

Place bag and joint onto a roasting rack with dish, to enable juices to drain away during cooking.

Cook in 2 stages:

a) on HIGH for 1 minute per lb.

b) on MEDIUM for 10-11 minutes per lb.

NB. The browning dish may be used to crisp crackling further.

Heat the dish with 1 tablespoon oil for 8-9 minutes on HIGH. Remove crackling from pork and add to hot dish.

Cook on HIGH for 2-4 minutes, turning once.

Roast Ham

Weigh ham, place on a rack, and cover during cooking. Cook in two stages:

a) on HIGH for 1 minute per lb.

b) on MEDIUM for 12-13 minutes per lb.

Apple Sauce

Remove the core from one large cooking apple and score the skin around the middle.

Cook in a deep bowl for 3-4 minutes on HIGH.

When cooked, remove the soft centre. Add sugar and serve.

Cheese Sauce

1 oz. cornflour
1 pint milk
2 oz. grated cheese

Add a little of the milk to the cornflour and mix thoroughly to a smooth paste.

Little by little, add the rest of the milk and the grated cheese, stirring gently.

Cook for 3 minutes on HIGH.

Remove and stir, then cook for a further 2-3 minutes on HIGH.

Roast Lamb

Weigh the joint, wash and pat dry.

Rub salt into the FAT only.

Place the joint in a roasting bag, sealing the end with an elastic band.

Pierce holes in the bag at the base.

Place bag and joint onto a roasting rack with dish, to enable juices to drain away during cooking.

Cook in 2 stages:

a) on HIGH for 1 minute per lb.

b) on MEDIUM for 10-11 minutes per lb.

NB. Reduce main cooking time if the joint is very small or has a high bone content.

Sprinkle the joint with rosemary before serving.

Sage & Onion Stuffing

Breadcrumbs from 8 slices of bread (no crusts)
1 medium onion (finely chopped).
3 heaped dessertspoons sage (dried and rubbed)
2 heaped dessertspoons suet (shredded)
1 egg (beaten)
Seasoning to taste

Cook the onions *(covered)* on HIGH for 2-3 minutes with a tablespoon of water.

Mix in remaining ingredients.

This mixture may be used for stuffing a turkey, or frozen.

Parsley & Thyme Stuffing

As above, but omitting the sage and adding $1\frac{1}{2}$ tablespoons each of dried parsley and thyme.

Scones

½ lb. self-raising flour
1 pinch of salt
½ teaspoon mixed spice
2 oz. margarine
2 oz. sugar (demerara gives better colour)
2 oz. mixed dried fruit
1 egg (beaten)
Milk to mix

Sift flour, salt and spices into a bowl.

Rub in margarine.

Stir in fruit and sugar, mixing with egg and enough milk to form a soft dough.

Knead lightly, roll into a shape 6″ in diameter.

Cut into 8 wedges.

Preheat browning dish for 5 minutes on HIGH.

Brush quickly with margarine.

Place scones in dish and cook for 1-1½ minutes on HIGH.

Turn scones over and cook for 2-2½ minutes on HIGH.

Flapjacks

3 tablespoons Golden Syrup
4 oz. demerara sugar
4 oz. butter/margarine
$\frac{1}{2}$ lb. rolled oats
1 teaspoon Baking Powder
$\frac{1}{2}$ teaspoon salt
1 egg (beaten)

Grease a 10" *(round)* flan dish.

Place syrup, sugar and butter into an oven-proof bowl and heat for 2-2$\frac{1}{2}$ minutes on HIGH.

Stir until sugar is dissolved.

Add remainder of ingredients and place in prepared container.

Cook for 3$\frac{1}{2}$-4-4$\frac{1}{2}$ minutes on HIGH.

Allow to stand before slicing.

Mince Pies

6 oz. self-raising flour
3 oz. soft margarine
1 tablespoon demerara sugar
1 egg (size 3)
Nutmeg
Milk
Extra demerara sugar

Rub margarine into flour to make crumbs.

Add sugar. Mix well with the egg to form pastry.

Roll out the pastry and use a large, circular cutter to cut out 18 shapes. Then use a smaller (biscuit size) cutter to cut out 18 "tops".

Grease a muffin pan and line with 6 of the larger shapes.

Cook on HIGH for 1½-2 minutes.

Put a teaspoon of mincemeat into each tartlet.

Cook on HIGH for 30-40 seconds more.

Repeat this operation with the remaining 12 tartlets.

Place the 18 "tops" on kitchen paper on a rack.

Cook on HIGH for 2 minutes. Place tops on tartlets.

NB: For the best-looking finish, brush the tops with milk and sprinkle them generously with demerara sugar and nutmeg before cooking.

Fruit Cake

3 oz. margarine
3 oz. brown sugar
2 eggs
4 oz. self-raising flour
8 oz. mixed fruit
1 teaspoon mixed spice
4 tablespoons milk

Blend margarine and sugar together thoroughly.

Beat the eggs separately and add one at a time, together with 1 tablespoon self-raising flour.

Stir in the mixed fruit. Add the milk and the other dry ingredients gradually, stirring to obtain a soft consistency with drops from the spoon.

Place mixture in a greased dish, approx. 8" diameter.

Cook for 6-6½ minutes on HIGH.

NB: For the best flavour, keep this cake for at least 24 hours before cutting.

Victoria Sponge

4 oz. self-raising flour
4 oz. soft margarine
4 oz. caster sugar
2 eggs (size 3)
2 tablespoons milk (to mix)

Prepare by creaming sugar and margarine together until soft and fluffy.

Add eggs, then fold in flour with the milk.

Divide mixture equally between two greased 8" sponge sandwich dishes.

Cook *each dish* for 2-2½ minutes on HIGH approx.

Turn out when cold and sandwich together with filling.

NB: Always grease the dishes.

Christmas Cake

4 oz. margarine

4 oz. dark brown sugar

2 eggs

$\frac{1}{2}$ tablespoon black treacle

2 oz. cherries (chopped)

1 oz. nuts (chopped)

1 lb. 6 oz. mixed fruit

Rind of $\frac{1}{2}$ lemon (grated)

Rind of $\frac{1}{2}$ orange (grated)

5 oz. plain flour

$\frac{1}{2}$ oz. cocoa

$1\frac{1}{2}$ teaspoons mixed spice

2 tablespoons milk or sherry

Cream sugar and butter until light and fluffy.

Beat together eggs and treacle.

Gradually add egg-and-treacle mixture to creamed mixture.

Wash cherries and toss in flour.

Mix in cherries, nuts and fruit.

Sieve together dry ingredients.

Fold in dry ingredients with sherry/milk.

Place in 8" or 9" greased, lined dish.

Cook on DEFROST setting for 40 mins *(approx)*.

Christmas Pudding

5 oz. plain flour

3 teaspoons mixed spice

6 oz. breadcrumbs

$\frac{1}{2}$ lb. soft brown sugar

$\frac{1}{2}$ lb. suet

1 lb. 6 oz. mixed dried fruit

2 oz. cherries (chopped)

2 oz. nuts (chopped)

Rind of 1 lemon (grated)

1 medium apple (grated)

4 eggs

3 tablespoons black treacle

2 tablespoons milk

$\frac{1}{4}$ pint stout

Mix all the ingredients together thoroughly.
Put into greased basins. Cover each basin with clingfilm, making 2 slits to prevent ballooning up.

Cook on HIGH { 1$\frac{1}{2}$ pint puddings: 7-8-9 minutes each.
1 pint puddings: 4$\frac{1}{2}$-5-6 minutes each.

Storage: Freeze if not required within 1 week.

Pineapple Upside-Down Pudding

4 oz. self-raising flour
4 oz. soft margarine
4 oz. caster sugar
2 eggs
Milk to mix
Demerara sugar
Small can pineapple rings (drain off juice)
4 glace cherries (halved)

Grease an 8" dish, sprinkle base with demerara sugar and arrange pineapple rings on top of sugar.

Place $\frac{1}{2}$ cherry in centre of each.

Make sponge mixture by creaming method (see "Victoria Sponge").

Put into dish on top of pineapple.

Cook for 5-5$\frac{1}{2}$-6 minutes on HIGH.

Turn upside down on plate to serve.

Rice Pudding

1 pint milk
2 oz. pudding rice
2 tablespoons sugar
Knob of butter
Pinch of nutmeg

Combine all the ingredients together in a large pie dish lightly greased with butter.

Cook for 5-6 minutes on HIGH, then 25-27 minutes on LOW.

Stir approx. every 10 minutes. Sprinkle nutmeg after 18 minutes cooking.

Apple Crumble

6 oz. self-raising flour
3 oz. soft brown sugar
3 oz. margarine
$\frac{3}{4}$ lb apples, peeled and sliced
Sugar to sweeten

Rub margarine into flour to form soft crumbs,
and stir in the brown sugar.
Place apples in a greased dish with sugar to taste.
Cover with crumble mixture.
Cook for 6-7 minutes on HIGH.

Steamed Sponge Pudding

4 oz. self-raising flour
4 oz. margarine
4 oz. caster sugar
2 eggs
4 tablespoons milk
3 tablespoons jam/golden syrup

Cream the sugar and margarine together, add the eggs, and then fold in the flour with the milk.

Put the syrup/jam in the bottom of a 2 pint greased dish, and place the mixture on top.

Cook for $4\frac{1}{2}$-5-$5\frac{1}{2}$ minutes on HIGH approx.

Mulled Wine

1 pint red wine
6 tablespoons brandy
1 stick of cinnamon
1 orange (or lemon), sliced
3 cloves
2 oz. sugar

Mix all the ingredients in a large bowl.
Heat for 5 minutes on HIGH.
Stir well. Serve warm, in glasses.

INDEX

Egg, scrambled 48
Fish, breaded 52
Fish cakes 40, 52
Fish fingers 40, 52
Flapjacks 83
Fruit cake 85
Garlic bread 71
Gravy 38
Haddock 40
Ham, roast 78
Kippers 40
Lamb, roast 80
Liver and bacon savoury 59
Macaroni cheese 74
Meat, joint 50
Meringue, quick 46
Milk 36
Mushrooms 42
Omelette 52
Onions 44
Parsnips 42
Pasty 54
Peas 44
Pie, fruit 54
Pie, meat 54
Pies, mince 84
Pineapple upside down pudding 89
Pizza 70
Pizza, ready-cooked 54
Pork, roast 78
Porridge 48
Potatoes, boiled 44
Potatoes, jacket 44
Pudding, rice 90
Pudding, tinned 54
Quiche, savoury 75
Rice, patna 48
Sausages 50
Scones 82